50 Life Lessons from Oprah Winfrey

Written by: George Ilian

Cover Illustration: Iren Flowers

Copyright © 2016

All Rights Reserved

Warning-Disclaimer

The purpose of this book is to educate and entertain. The author or publisher does not guarantee that anyone following the techniques, suggestions, tips, ideas, or strategies will become successful. The author and publisher shall have neither liability or responsibility to anyone with respect to any loss or damage caused or alleged to be caused, directly or indirectly by the information contained in this book.

More Books By George Ilian

George Ilian is the author of many inspirational books and guides how to make money online.

His mission is to help you have all the money and freedom you need to go and live anywhere you want and travel around the world. It is all possible with the money that you can make online, giving you the ability to have everything you've ever wanted—and more!

50 Lessons in Life and Business you can Learn from Oprah Winfrey

If there is a queen of chat shows in the USA, it is Oprah Winfrey. This self-made billionaire is far more than a talking head, however: she has leveraged her public profile to make a $3 billion fortune. She is the richest African American, and greatest black philanthropist, in history. Oprah has honorary doctorates from both Duke and Harvard Universities, and in 2013 President Barack Obama awarded her the Presidential Medal of Freedom. Her rise from childhood poverty in rural Mississippi, and her teenage years as a single mother in inner city Milwaukee, having become pregnant aged just 14, is nothing short of a miracle. Even in fairytales, heroines don't triumph over adversity like this.

Be thankful for what you have; you'll end up having more. If you concentrate on what you don't have, you will never, ever have enough.

Oprah Winfrey

So what is it that has enabled Oprah Winfrey to succeed when countless others have fallen by the wayside? What are her personal attributes, how does she position herself, and what is it that drives her to go on? Having come from nowhere, with no obvious advantages in life, the lessons she can teach us are invaluable. If someone as disadvantaged in life as Oprah Winfrey can go on to achieve the things she has, such possibilities are open to any one of us. She is the ultimate role model, an inspiration whether you are black or white, female or male, rich or poor.

Oprah Winfrey has been in the public limelight for more than 40 years, and her life was not uneventful before that. In this book we will examine the key periods of her life, the events which made her the women she is today, and endeavour to extract from them key lessons which you can apply in your own life and business. Some of these lessons will be complex, and require time to think about. Other will be simple, and you can begin to action them straight away. We have highlighted these bite-sized lessons throughout the book so that if you are short of time, you can spot them quickly, returning to read each chapter in more detail at a later date.

Chapter 1 examines Oprah's childhood and education, the period which probably most shaped her as a person, and which undoubtedly was the most difficult in her life. It describes what happened to Oprah, and what she did about it, before she began her career in television.

Chapter 2 looks at Oprah's television career, from co-anchoring local news channels, to being the face of the most successful talk show in the history of American broadcasting: *The Oprah Winfrey Show*. Oprah's personality, her insight into guests and viewers alike, and her desire to use her television platform for good, all shine through. This is followed by *Chapter 3: Other Media Projects*, a discussion of her publishing, film, radio, and online initiatives, many of which were spin-offs from her television show, but which have not always been commercial successes. Oprah's business empire - the company structures which own and create her numerous products - is explored in *Chapter 4*.

After this, the book then shifts away from Oprah's career to examine in detail her awards and honours (*Chapter 5*) her philanthropic efforts, in the US and overseas (*Chapter 6*); and her thought leadership and influence over the American public (*Chapter 7*). This chapter considers in particular Oprah's ability to change public ideas on contemporary issues such as homosexuality, her ability to influence the outcome of political elections, and the impact that her endorsements have on the sale consumer items.

Oprah's private life, including her early relationships and long-term partnership with Stedman Graham, is discussed in

Chapter 8. The book finishes with a conclusion, summarising the most important lessons which Oprah can, and would want to, teach us.

Chapter 1: Childhood and Education

Few people's formative years are bleaker than those of Oprah Winfrey. She was born on January 29, 1954 in Kosciusko, Mississippi to Vernita Lee, an unmarried teenage housemaid, who had conceived her daughter on a one-night stand with a coal miner turned barber scarcely older than she was. The child was named Orpah on her birth certificate, a biblical name suggested by her aunt, which was taken from the Book of Ruth. None of her relatives knew how to spell the name when they wrote it down, and in any case, anyone who saw it from then on always mispronounced it as Oprah. This inadvertent moniker stuck.

Oprah grew up in desperate poverty. Her mother left to look for work shortly after she was born, and Oprah was cared for by her grandmother, Hattie Mae Lee. The family's situation was such that Oprah wore dresses made from potato sacks, which even in the impoverished society where she lived marked her out as different. She was inevitably bullied for her appearance by her peers.

Lesson 1: Economic poverty, however desperate, can be overcome. Just because you start with nothing does not mean that you are fated to always be poor.

Young Oprah was smart, however, and by the age of three, her grandmother had already taught her to read. She had a good memory and a strong voice, so the congregation at the local church nicknamed her "the Preacher".

Lesson 2: Early years education is vital to success later in life. Whatever your financial position, invest in the education of your children from the very start.

Oprah's mother came back into her life when Oprah was six, uprooting her from her grandmother's home and moving her to Milwaukee. Vernita Lee worked interminable hours for minimal pay, and had little time for her daughter. She gave birth to a second daughter, Patricia, and sent Oprah away once again, this time to be cared for by her biological father, Vernon Winfrey. During her absence, two more children were born: another daughter, who was put up for adoption for financial reasons; and a son.

Not even having reached puberty, Oprah was molested by a relatives, notably a cousin and an uncle, and also by a family friend. When she attempted to raise the abuse with her immediate family, years later, they refused to accept what she said, and it was not until 1986, on one of her own programmes about sexual abuse, that Oprah felt able to talk about what had happened to her publicly. In any case, the emotional and psychological damage of these years was permanent: Oprah told an interviewer on the BBC News that the reason she had chosen not to be a mother because she herself had not been mothered well.

Lesson 3: The repercussions of physical and emotional abuse will last a lifetime. Although you might be able to function, and even to thrive, that does not remove the underlying scars.

Aged just 13, Oprah ran away from home. She became pregnant at 14, but her son was born prematurely, and died not long after he was born. Oprah was, regardless, just a child herself, with no capacity to care for a baby. Having returned to live with her mother, Oprah attended Lincoln High School, and then the more affluent Nicolet High School, but she was acutely aware of her poverty, and felt it was constantly rubbed in her face by her peers. Oprah fell into a bad crowd, and stole money to keep up appearances.

The struggle of my life created empathy - I could relate to pain, being abandoned, having people not love me.

Oprah Winfrey

Again, Vernita Lee sent Oprah to live with her father, but this time the arrangement was much more of a success. Vernon Winfrey valued education, and made it a priority for Oprah. He sent her to East Nashville Hill School, where she quickly found her feet. She joined the high school speech team, and won a prestigious oratory competition, the prize for which was a full scholarship to study communication at Tennessee State University. Education gave Oprah the spring-board she needed to leave Milwaukee, her poverty, and many of her troubles, behind.

Where there is no struggle, there is no strength.

Oprah Winfrey

Lesson 4: Education is the single most important means of creating ambition, and the means by which those ambitions can be realised.

Chapter 2: Television Career

Whilst she was still a student, Oprah began putting her communication skills to work. She presented the news part time at WVOL, a Nashville-based radio station which broadcast predominantly to Tennessee's African-American community. On graduating, the moved to WLAC-TV (a CBS-affiliated TV station), also in Nashville, and became their first black female news anchor. Oprah was also the youngest news anchor hired by the channel.

Lesson 5: Youth need not be a drawback to achievement. If you have energy, and are good at what you do, opportunities will avail themselves.

The late 1970s saw Oprah move through a succession of jobs in local television news, first to anchor the six o'clock news at WJZ-TV in Baltimore, and then to co-host the channel's local talk show, *People Are Talking*, and *Dialing for Dollars*. Oprah's warmth and enthusiasm engaged listeners and viewers alike, and having a young, dynamic black woman on screen was something fresh, which appealed to channel executives.

Oprah's big break, her leap from local broadcasting to a national stage, occurred in 1983 when she was headhunted by WLS-TV in Chicago. She took over their morning talk show, *AM Chicago*, and in a matter of months transformed it from a low-performing programme, to the highest rated talk show in Chicago. All eyes were on Oprah to see what she would do next.

Lesson 6: You can't sit at home and expect opportunities to pop up there. You need to be prepared to move, sometimes long distances, in order to take the next step.

One of those watching closely was film critic Roger Ebert. He convinced Oprah to sign a syndication contract with King World, and her morning talk show was renamed *The Oprah Winfrey Show*. Fans now turned on the box for an hour every morning, entranced by her intelligence and sassiness, and when national broadcasting of the show began in September 1986, it quickly became the number-one daytime talk show in America. Writing at the time in TIME magazine, journalist Richard Zoglin was to the point:

> Few people would have bet on Oprah Winfrey's swift rise to host of the most popular talk show on TV. In a field dominated by white males, she is a black female of ample bulk. [...] What she lacks in journalistic toughness, she makes up for in plainspoken curiosity, robust humor and, above all empathy. Guests with sad stories to tell

are apt to rouse a tear in Oprah's eye [...] They, in turn, often find themselves revealing things they would not imagine telling anyone, much less a national TV audience. It is the talk show as a group therapy session.

The Oprah Winfrey Show was broadcast nationally from 1986 until 2011, making it one of the longest running daytime talk shows in history. Initially tabled as a tabloid talk show, Oprah went on to make the programme a platform for her educational and philanthropic initiatives too.

With viewer figures estimated to have reached 20 million a day at the peak of the show's popularity, everyone who was everyone wanted to make an appearance, and Oprah had no shortage of celebrity guests. CBS Anchor and Oprah's best friend, Gayle King, made a record 141 appearances on the show, and singer Celine Dion clocked up 28. Oprah interviewed Tom Cruise, Elizabeth Taylor, and even Michael Jackson. That interview, filmed at the singer's home, Neverland, and broadcast live, was watched by 90 million people, making it the most-watched television interview in history.

Lesson 7: People are interested in celebrities, and want to hear what they have to say. Surrounding yourself with celebrities is a good way to increase your own popularity.

But Oprah wasn't only interested in the lives of the rich and famous: she was fascinated by the lives of ordinary people too, and wanted to bring their experiences to light, prompting discussion amongst her audiences. She interviewed the parents of murdered children, those with life-threatening and incurable diseases, and the victims of abuse. It was in one such interview, with a woman named Trudie Chase in the show's 1989-90 season, that Oprah broke down on hearing about her guest's violent sexual abuse, and then recounted her own experiences of childhood molestation (see *Chapter 1: Childhood and Education*). Oprah invited 200 men who had been victims of childhood abuse to appear on an episode during the show's final season, along with director and producer Tyler Perry, himself an abuse survivor, in the hope that it would encourage other victims to realise they did not have to suffer in silence and in shame, but could be open about what the had endured, and bring the perpetrators to justice.

Real integrity is doing the right thing, knowing that nobody's going to know whether you did it or not.

Oprah Winfrey

Lesson 8: The stories of ordinary people can be just as enthralling as those of the famous. Don't ever discount someone, or their experiences, because you think they are too mundane.

Oprah knew early on that her show was about more than just entertainment. By discussing prominent issues of current affairs, such as gun crime, racism, mental illness, or abuse, she could change public attitudes. She also realised the show could be a tool for educating middle America, and because of this, she created *Oprah's Book Club*.

Originally a segment of *The Oprah Winfrey Show*, each month Oprah would select a book (usually a novel) to discuss on air. Four of the books she featured generated multi-million sales, and they invariably shot straight to the top of the best-sellers lists, even if they had been originally published years before. Eckhard Tolle's *A New Earth* sold 3,370,000 copies after being included on Oprah's reading list in 2008. Oprah combined her book discussions with author interviews and other related features, including a visit to the Auschwitz concentration camp with Elie Wiesel, an author, Holocaust survivor, and Nobel Laureate.

Lesson 9: Entertainment and education can go hand in hand, and when new information is delivered in an engaging format, people are more keen to learn.

In her book, *Reading with Oprah: The Book Club That Changed America*, writer and publisher Kathleen Rooney described Oprah as being, "a serious American intellectual who pioneered the use of electronic media, specifically television and the Internet, to take reading—a decidedly non-technological and highly individual act—and highlight its social elements and uses in such a way to motivate millions of erstwhile non-readers to pick up books." *Business Week* was similarly impressed with the leverage Oprah had on the publishing industry, claiming, "No one comes close to Oprah's clout: Publishers estimate that her power to sell a book is anywhere from 20 to 100 times that of any other media personality."

Books were my pass to personal freedom. I learned to read at age three, and soon discovered there was a whole world to conquer that went beyond our farm in Mississippi.

Oprah Winfrey

Lesson 10: Learning should be a life-long process. What-
ever your age, and whatever your situation, you are never
too old or too busy to learn something new.

Oprah also used *The Oprah Winfrey Show* to reach out
to audiences, encouraging them to improve their health
and well-being, and to increase their aspirations. Having come herself from such impoverished, desperate
beginnings, she knew the importance of role models,
and that she herself could set an example to others.
We'll discuss her leadership and influence more in
Chapter 7, but here we can specifically consider her
talk show's self-help elements.

Lesson 11: People in positions of power, and influence,
have a moral responsibility to educate the people who look
up to them, and to set a positive example.

Although Oprah's own opinions held great weight with
her television audiences, she understood that for important matters such as health, finance, and marital issues, it gave the show credibility if she brought on experts in their respective fields. Iyanla Vanzant, life
coach and spiritual teacher, began appearing on the
show in the late 1990s, advising mostly on relationship
issues, and in 2000, *Ebony* magazine rated her as one

of the "100 most influential Black Americans". Dr. Phil McGraw ("Dr Phil"), a psychologist from Oklahoma, used his academic background to give advice on relationships, bad habits, bad attitudes, and weight loss, and his spin-off show, *Dr. Phil*, began in 2002. Last year, *Forbes* magazine ranked him the 15th highest earning celebrity in the world. It is a similar success story for financial expert Suze Orman, who spoke on the show about credit card debt, budgeting, etc.

The greatest discovery of all time is that a person can change his future by merely changing his attitude.

Oprah Winfrey

Lesson 12: Your professional relationships should be mutually beneficial. If someone else's efforts add to your own credibility, you should give them a leg-up in return.

The Oprah Winfrey Show ran until 2011. The 25th season was Oprah's last, but my was it impressive: Oprah flew all 300 audience members to Australia, with John Travolta as the pilot; she interviewed President Barack Obama and First Lady Michelle Obama; and the final episode included appearances from Arethra Franklin, Tom Cruise, Stevie Wonder, Will Smith, and Beyonce. Hundreds of graduates who had received the Oprah Winfrey Scholarship at Morehouse College were in the audience, and the show received its highest ratings figures in 17 years. Oprah's own feelings about this end of an era were frank, and generally celebratory. She said to her viewers:

> I've been asked many times during this farewell season, 'Is ending the show bittersweet?' Well, I say all sweet. No bitter. And here is why: Many of us have been together for 25 years. We have hooted and hollered together, had our aha! moments, we ugly-cried together and we did our gratitude journals. So I thank you all for your support and your trust in me. I thank you for sharing this yellow brick road of blessings. I thank you for tuning in every day along with your mothers and your sisters and your daughters, your partners, gay and otherwise, your friends and all the husbands who got coaxed into watching *Oprah*. And I thank you for being as much of a sweet inspiration for me as I've tried to be for you. I won't say goodbye. I'll just say...until we meet again. To God be the glory.

During the show's lifetime, it received 47 Daytime Emmy Awards, eight GLAAD Media Awards, five Image Awards, and a TV Guide Award. In 2013, TV Guide also ranked *The Oprah Winfrey Show* as the 19th greatest show of all time.

Lesson 13: Even the greatest projects have a natural shelf life. One of the hardest things in business is to anticipate when that end is nigh, and to draw things to a close grace-fully.

Chapter 3: Other Media Projects

By the mid 1980s, Oprah Winfrey was already a household name, and this meant that she had her pick of other media projects. She was savvy in those she chose, however, always selecting opportunities which furthered her career, or related to issues she cared about.

Films Oprah made her big screen debut in *The Color Purple* in 1985. Directed by Steven Spielberg, this period drama was an adaptation of the novel of the same name. The film's themes of poverty, racism, and sexism in the southern United States must have resonated with Oprah. The film was a box office success, earning $142 million worldwide, and it was favourably received by critics: the online review site *Rotten Tomatoes* amalgamates critics' reviews to give the film an overall score of 88%, and describes it as "a sentimental tale that reveals great emotional truths in American history." Oprah appeared in the film as Sofia Johnson, the daughter-in-law of the film's female protagonist, who is herself a victim of sexual abuse, but refuses to be cowed by her attackers.

The themes of *The Color Purple* are also evident in some of Oprah's later films. She appeared as Sethe, a former slave living in Cincinati in the aftermath of the American civil war, in the 1998 horror-drama *Beloved*; and in 2005 she was the executive producer for *Their Eyes Were Watching God*, a television movie based on Zora Neale Hurston's novel, itself considered to be a seminal work of African-American fiction. Her preparations for her role in *Beloved* were particularly thorough and harrowing: she was tied up, blindfolded and left alone in the woods to have an idea of what it must have been like to be a slave.

Lesson 14: If you want something to be a success, you have to give it your all. This is much easier if it is something you truly believe in.

Harpo Productions (see *Chapter 4: Business Empire*) also developed and produced a number of films and documentaries for HBO, and Oprah made small appearances, often as a voice-over artist, in children's cartoons. She voiced Gussie the goose in *Charlotte's Web*, Judge Bumbledon in the *Bee Movie*, and also recorded the voice of Eudora in Disney's *The Princess and the Frog*.

Magazines Oprah published two magazines, *O at Home*, and *O, The Oprah Magazine*, which *Fortune* declared to be the most successful ever start-up in the publishing industry.

O, The Oprah Magazine, abbreviated as *O*, was first published in 2000, and is targeted primarily at middle-aged, female readers - the same sort of people who watched *The Oprah Winfrey Show*. Oprah appears on every cover, sometimes accompanied by other high-profile women such as Michelle Obama and Ellen DeGeneres, and topics covered in the magazine include fashion and beauty, health, finances, and books. It is intended to project Oprah's opinions and style, and her image and comments are present throughout.

The paid circulation of *O* peaked in 2004, at 2.7 million copies. Although most magazines experienced declining print sales in the late 2000s, *O* held strong in the marketplace. Today, the magazine's circulation hovers around 2.4 million copies, two-thirds of which are sold by subscription, and the rest through news stands. Nearly 2/3 of readers are Caucasian, and the balance African-American, Hispanic, and Asian. The digital issue of the magazine was launched in 2010, for iPad users, and the app gives readers access to videos and the ability to purchase books from Oprah's book list.

Lesson 15: If you are lucky enough to create a product which people want to buy in to, be prepared to spin it in dif-

ferent ways. Give your fans (your customers) a variety of products to choose from.

O at Home was a spin-off from *O, The Oprah Magazine*, was published by the Hearst Corporation, and after it was launched in 2004, it quickly grew to have a circulation of 1.4 million. *O at Home* was published quarterly, and focused on home furnishings, decorating tips, and good interior design on a budget. The magazine closed in 2008, as Hearst tried to cut costs in the face of falling advertising revenues, and its content themes were reincorporated into *O, The Oprah Magazine*.

Think like a queen. A queen is not afraid to fail. Failure is another steppingstone to greatness.

Oprah Winfrey

Lesson 16: There is no shame in failing: it is a natural part of learning and developing. If something does not work out, for whatever reason, try something else instead.

Books To date, Oprah has co-written five books, on a variety of topics.

In 1996, writing with Bill Adler, Oprah released *The Uncommon Wisdom of Oprah Winfrey: A Portrait in Her*

Own Words. The moving story of her early life and rise to fame, in the book she explores themes of family, success, weight loss, relationships, as well as her own pains, passions, and ambitions. Her views and insight are provided in the form of quotes, which Adler then elaborates on.

Lesson 17: Play to your strengths, and let others play to theirs. It is perfectly acceptable to delegate responsibility to other people, especially if they can do something better than you can.

Capitalising on interest in the self-help field, which itself developed in no small part due to *The Oprah Winfrey Show*, Oprah co-wrote *Make The Connection: 10 Steps To A Better Body And A Better Life* with personal trainer, Bob Greene. This book was also published in 1996. In the book, Oprah is blunt about her own struggles with weight - she had tried, and failed at, every diet imaginable - but the book then shifts to looking at how Greene helped her to lose (and largely keep off) more than 70 lbs by eating more healthily and exercising regularly. The 10 steps referred to in the book's title are the core of Greene's weight loss programme, and include ways to increase your metabolism. Oprah's own story runs alongside these practical tips, providing encouragement through inspiration. Though the book is now 20 years old, it is still well-reviewed by dieters, many of whom return to Oprah and Greene's advice again and again.

Lesson 18: Partnering with an expert in a specific field is the best way to create a quality product, and thus increase the likelihood that your project will succeed.

Journey to Beloved was published two years later, in 1998. Written by Oprah and with photographs by Ken Regan, it is the story of how Oprah fell in love with Toni Morrison's Pulitzer Prize-winning novel, *Beloved*, and decided to make it into a film (see *Films*, above). The book is principally a production diary, with an essay to preface it, but even in this somewhat sterile format, we see Oprah's emotions and vulnerabilities. She is filled with doubts about her ability to play her character, Sethe. Even in the company of so many experienced film makers, she worries that she lacks the skill and strength to pull the project off. And Oprah clearly feels a great weight of responsibility to do justice to the book, its characters, themes, and the real people who have inspired it, writing:

Tomorrow is the first day of dialogue. Am I ready? I think so. I bring the force and grace of history and pain with me, carrying the Ancestors in my heart, hoping, but also knowing, they, too, carry me.... I ask God for grace, and the power of the spirits whose lives went unnoticed, demeaned and diminished by slavery. Calling on you. Calling on you. I try to prepare in terms of logic, reasoning, what would [Sethe] be thinking - chronologically - but I really believe I can call her up. Her and so many others. I'm counting on them.

Those who have read the book are often moved by Oprah's accounts to read the original novel, or to watch the film.

Lesson 19: People don't buy products, they buy emotions. When you are creating something, you therefore need to be aware of how it will make people feel.

The most recent of Oprah's books is *What I Know For Sure*, published in 2014. Originally the title of her column in *O, The Oprah Magazine* (see *Magazines*, above), this book is a cloth-bound collection of the best of her columns, many of which have been specially revised and updated. Candid and moving, uplifting and frequently funny, the essays provide insight into the way that Oprah thinks and feels. The essays are arranged by theme - joy, resilience, connection, gratitude, possibility, awe, clarity, and power - and are intended to help readers to define their ambitions, work towards realising them, and be fulfilled. Oprah combines her own experiences with messages for others, for example:

My highest achievement: never shutting down my heart. Even in my darkest moments—through sexual abuse, a pregnancy at 14, lies and betrayals—I remained faithful, hopeful, and willing to see the best in people, regardless of whether they were showing me their worst. I continued to believe that no matter how hard the climb, there is always a way to let in a sliver of light to illuminate the path forward.

Lesson 20: Adding your own opinions and experiences to your products adds authenticity, and is an effective means of marketing.

Unlike some celebrities, who seem to have a new, ghost-written book out every other week, Oprah has held off on publishing a second memoir or autobiography for many years. Perhaps she was just too busy, or perhaps she felt that she had more to achieve before putting pen to paper. In any case, having retired from *The Oprah Winfrey Show*, she had more time, and thus began to write. Her forthcoming memoir, entitled *The Life You Want*, will look at Oprah's own life, and also give inspirational advice: much like this book, in fact! *The Life You Want* is scheduled for publication by Flatiron Books in 2017, and critics are already chomping at the bit to read it. Writing in the *New York Times* in December 2015, Alexandra Alter has already predicted that Oprah's memoir will be the best-selling book of the year.

Lesson 21: Building suspense is a very effective marketing tool. Work out what your customers want, and dangle it just out of reach, and they will want it even more.

Radio *Oprah Radio* (originally called *Oprah and Friends*) was a talk-show radio channel which ran from 2006 to 2014. Oprah's first three year contract with the station's owners, XM Satellite Radio, was said to be worth $55 million.

Broadcast from Oprah's own studio in Chicago, the channel featured not only Oprah, but also key figures who frequently appeared on *The Oprah Winfrey Show*, such as personal trainer Bob Greene, interior designer Nate Berkus, cardiothoracic surgeon and alternative medicine support Dr. Mehmet Cengiz Öz ("Dr. Oz"), and spiritual teacher Marianne Williamson. Oprah was contractually to be on the air 30 minutes a week, 39 weeks a year, and she often presented her segment along with CBS anchor Gayle King.

Lesson 22: Every business has key personnel. Understand who they are, work out what you need from them, and how you can keep them engaged.

The topics discussed on *Oprah Radio* were very similar to those on *The Oprah Winfrey Show*: current affairs, self-improvement, health, nutrition, fitness, relationships, and tips for your home all featured. The channel was broadcast by a number of companies in succession, but ceased broadcasting on 31 December, 2014. Listeners were not informed of the channel's shutdown in advance.

Do the one thing you think you cannot do. Fail at it. Try again. Do better the second time. The only people who never tumble are those who never mount the high wire. This is your moment. Own it.

Oprah Winfrey

Lesson 23: Even the most successful entrepreneurs sometimes make flawed decisions. The important thing is not that you failed, but that you get back up and try something else.

Online Presence In order to coordinate all her activities, and to create a hub where fans to access everything in one place, Oprah created **oprah.com**. According to Quantcast, the website currently receives 4.8 million unique visitors every month (down from 6 million in 2008), 70% of whom are in the US. The vast majority of visitors to the site are women in the 35-65 age bracket, and by far the largest ethnic group of users is African-American.

oprah.com is a mine of information, and thankfully well organised enough that you can usually find what you are looking for. The latest stories from *O, The Oprah Magazine*, are on the home page, along with advertisements for courses, events, and branded products available from the *O Store*, Oprah's online shop. The home page also includes some video content, and an invitation for readers to share their own experiences on a variety of topics, so that they feel engaged. The topics - everything from *Dads: Is your ex blocking you from your child?* to *Are you a Caribbean woman who feels shunned?* and *Are you an ex-con who can't seem to catch a break?* - are all slightly sensationalist, encouraging readers to read and comment on what others have said, even if they have nothing to contribute themselves.

Lesson 24: Engaging your customers and building a sense of rapport with them increases their sense of loyalty to your brand.

The bulk of the website's content is divided into several dozen different categories, all of which are accessible from the side bar menu. These include common topics such as *Fashion & Beauty*, *Food*, *Health & Wellness*, and *Inspiration*, but also special sections for all of Oprah's courses, and television shows produced by the Oprah Winfrey Network (OWN, see *Chapter 4: Business Empire*). The website has a dedicated discussion area (*Community Conversations*), an area for competitions and promotions (*Sweepstakes*), and also a book store tied in with Oprah's Book Club (see *Chapter 2: Television Career*).

The *Books* section is one of the most interesting parts of oprah.com: it is at once a valuable information source which promotes Oprah's educational objectives, and also a lucrative money spinner. Numerous book lists are provided under the *Reading Room*, and all of them can be purchased online, generating oprah.com a referral fee from the vendors. A second income stream is generated through advertising: pay-per-click adverts, typically for products and services unrelated to the book, appear beneath each book review.

Lesson 25: Your business' website has two purposes: to inform customers, and to make money. Both of these purposes go hand in hand, and you should not overlook one in favour of the other.

Chapter 4: Business Empire

What I know is, is that if you do work that you love, and the work fulfils you, the rest will come.

Oprah Winfrey

Oprah is acutely aware that she herself is a multi-billion dollar brand: people want to hear what she says and thinks, and she can capitalise on this, through endorsements and advertising, to make mega bucks. A single tweet from Oprah's Twitter account, for example, is thought to have boosted Weight Watchers' earnings by $150 million.

Lesson 26: Your brand, and that of your company, are intimately linked. You should therefore think about your personal and professional platforms as one and the same.

Although she is personally shrewd, she has also been very well advised throughout her career, enabling her to make the best business decisions. The fact that *Forbes* magazine currently estimates her net wealth at $3.1 billion, is testament to this fact. Unlike many of her wealthy peers, she has not inherited a cent, but made it entirely herself.

Lesson 27: The easiest way to become a millionaire is to inherit it. If you aren't lucky enough to be in that position, however, you can still reach the same levels of wealth, it is just much harder work.

In *Chapter 2: Television Career* and *Chapter 3: Other Media Projects*, we have talked about the products Oprah has created, for film and television, publishing and radio, and online. In this chapter, then, we will look at the commercial vehicles which have enabled her to build her business empire, to promote herself on so many different platforms, and to capitalise, professional and financially, on all of them.

It is easy to think of Oprah as a talk show host, a celebrity, but she is a businesswoman first and fore-most. Indeed, Nicole Aschoff, writing in The Guardian, went as far as to describe her as, "one of the world's best neoliberal capitalist thinkers." Oprah embodies the American Dream, although, as Aschoff is at pains to point out, for most people:

> [the American Dream] is a fiction. If all or most forms of social and cultural capital were equally valuable and accessible, we should see the effects of this in increased upward mobility and wealth created anew by new people in each generation rather than passed down and expanded from one generation to

the next. The data do not demonstrate this upward mobility.

In any case, we still aspire to be like Oprah. Reality, however brutal, does not blunt our dreams, and a role model like Oprah - someone who has made it against all the odds - just makes us work harder to try and realise them.

The biggest adventure you can take is to live the life of your dreams.

Oprah Winfrey

Lesson 28: The American Dream is, for most people, just a dream, something which they aspire towards, but will never reach. For a lucky few, however, that dream can become a reality.

Oprah's business empire is managed, and expanded, by two companies, Harpo Productions, and the Oprah Winfrey Network (OWN).

Harpo Productions Founded in Chicago in 1986, Harpo Productions (the sole subsidiary of Harpo, Inc.) employs more than 12,000 people and handles the bulk of Oprah's business empire. The name, Harpo, is Oprah spelt backwards, but was also the name of Oprah's on-screen husband in *The Color Purple* (see *Films*, in *Chapter 3: Other Media Projects*).

Lesson 29: Choose a business name which is catchy, and ideally which means something to you.

Each of Oprah's business areas forms a subsidiary of Harpo Productions, though not all of those subsidiaries are still operational.

Harpo Print, in partnership with Hearst Magazines, publishes *O, The Oprah Magazine* (see *Magazines* in *Chapter 3: Other Media Projects*) and also the now-defunct *O Home*.

Harpo Films, founded in 1993, was once the largest division of Harpo Productions, and it developed and produced motion pictures and long-form television programmes. Harpo Films had an overlap of interests with Harpo Studios, the home of *The Oprah Winfrey Show* in Chicago, and where many of her other film and television projects, including *Beloved*, were filmed. Harpo Films closed in 2013, but with most of its staff moving to Harpo Studio and OWN (see below).

Harpo Studies now controls much of Oprah's television output, plus that of the protégés whose careers she has helped to launch. In addition to producing *The*

Oprah Winfrey Show (1986-2011), Harpo Studios also produces *Dr. Phil* (2002-present), *Rachael Ray* (2006-present), *The Dr. Oz Show* (2009-present), and many more. Oprah's own shows, notably *Oprah Prime, Oprah: Where Are They Now?, Oprah's Master Class*, and *Oprah's Life Class*, are all products belonging to Harpo Studios.

Harpo Radio was the holding company for *Oprah Radio* (see *Radio* in *Chapter 3: Other Media Projects*), which ran from 2006 to 2014.

Harpo Productions also owns oprah.com (see *Online* in *Chapter 3: Other Media Projects*).

Lesson 30: Take expert advice and think carefully about how to structure your own business enterprises. It is sometimes necessary to spread risk, and liability, between multiple legal entities.

The Oprah Winfrey Network (OWN) The Oprah Winfrey Network (OWN) is an offshoot of Harpo Productions (see above), though it too is an umbrella for multiple different projects. Founded in 2011, the company has two stakeholders, Harpo Productions and Discovery Communications, both of which own 50%.

OWN is a television channel, available to 82 million households in the US, and its content is also syndicated to TLC UK (UK), Discovery Home & Health (Australia), DStv (South Africa), and local channels in Bulgaria, Poland, Romania, and Russia. Its viewing ratings - averaging 581,000 in the first quarter of 2015 - are reasonable when compared to OWN's competitors, but a fraction of the 7 million viewers Oprah herself could expect to attract during a particularly juicy episode of *The Oprah Winfrey Show*. The network's viewing figures are generally boosted by one-off occasions when a celebrity comes on a show and what they say makes breaking news: disgraced Tour de France winner Lance Armstrong's public confession that he had used performance enhancing drugs attracted 4.3 million viewers; and Oprah's interview with Bobbi Kristina Brown, broadcast a month to the day after her mother Whitney Houston's death by drowning, broke even that record.

Lesson 31: Exclusivity is a very powerful marketing tool: it makes people want what you have. Work to find something which no one else can give your customers, and they will then flock to you.

OWN broadcasts a mixture of talk shows and films, both original series and re-runs of popular shows.

Much of the content is broadcast as marathons - back to back episodes of the same programme - and the majority of shows broadcast are products of Harpo Studios (see above). All of Oprah's own shows are broadcast on the channel, as are those of Nate Berkus, Rachael Ray, and Dr. Phil. Tyler Perry, one of the highest paid performers in the US, signed a contract with OWN in 2012 to produce 90 episodes of original content, and to broadcast all his new material through the channel. His series, which include *The Haves and the Have Nots*, and *Love Thy Neighbor*, have been great commercial successes, and so the partnership was renewed. Perry's viewer figures actually now exceed those of Oprah herself.

Lesson 32: Successful products don't have to be original. You can rework, and redistribute, existing products in multiple ways, and still make money doing so.

Chapter 5: Awards and Honours

Oprah's awards and honours are almost too numerous to count: if there is a prize in existence, she has probably already won it, or at least been nominated.

In *Chapter 2: Television Career*, we discussed some of the awards won by *The Oprah Winfrey Show* which, of course, was made possible by Oprah herself. As an individual presenter, she also received the People's Choice Award on four separate occasions across three decades (1988, 1997, 1998, and 2004), she was twice nominated for Academy Awards for her film roles (1986 and 2015), she was given a Lifetime Achievement Award by the Emmy Awards (1998), and in 2005 she was inducted into the National Association for the Advancement of Colored People (NAACP) Hall of Fame in recognition of her work in television and film.

Lesson 33: Gaining recognition within your industry is an effective way to raise your business' profile, as other people will publicise your achievements on your behalf.

Oprah's awards stretch beyond the worlds of film and television, however: she was honoured with the Jefferson Award for Public Service in 1998, and the Peabody Award, also for meritorious public service, in 1995.

Oprah received the Bob Hope Humanitarian Award in 2002, and the Kennedy Center Honors in 2010.

There is one award, however, which Oprah is more proud of than all the others, and rightly so. On November 22, 2013, Oprah was invited to the White House, where President Barack Obama presented her with the Presidential Medal of Freedom, the highest civilian award of the United States. The award recognises those who have made "an especially meritorious contribution to the security or national interests of the United States, world peace, cultural or other significant public or private endeavors," and as a recipient, Oprah follows in the footsteps of the Apollo 13 crew, Mother Teresa, and scientist Stephen Hawking.

Lesson 34: If you excel in your field, whatever it is, and campaign tirelessly for issues you believe in, you and your efforts will ultimately come to wider attention.

Chapter 6: Philanthropy

Acutely aware of where she has come from, and the potential which her personal wealth has to change lives, Oprah is an active philanthropist. In fact, *Businessweek* records that she became the first black person to rank among the 50 most generous Americans, and by 2012 she had already given away $400 million to educational causes alone. She has donated more than 400 scholarships to Morehouse College in Atlanta, Georgia, and in 2013 made a one-off donation of $12 million to the Smithsonian's National Museum of African American History and Culture.

Lesson 35: No one achieves wealth, or greatness, on their own. If you make money, you have a moral obligation to give something back to the communities which have enabled you to excel.

Oprah create Oprah's Angel Network in 1998 to support charitable projects and provide grants to NGOs. She personally covered all administrative costs of the network, and so every cent of the $80 million it raised went to the front line of charities' work. This included a donation of $11 million ($10 million of which was a personal donation from Oprah) for relief efforts in the wake of Hurricanes Katrina and Rita, which devastated predominantly poor, black communities in Texas, Missis-sippi, Louisiana, and Alabama.

Lesson 36: Sometimes the most effective gift you can give is not your money, but your time, platform, and endorsement. Leverage your position to encourage others to support causes you believe in.

The philanthropic project which Oprah is most proud of, however, is the Oprah Winfrey Leadership Academy for Girls, close to Johannesburg in South Africa. The root of the idea formed in 2000 when Oprah was a guest of Nelson Mandela at his home in Western Cape. The pair discussed poverty at some length, and agreed that education was the best way of giving poor South African youths - and girls in particular - a chance to im-prove their lives.

Oprah initially pledged $10 million for a school, and began developing a state-of-the-art campus. Her finan-cial commitment increased to $40 million as the scope of the project grew. She began recruiting students in 2006, stipulating that only the brightest but most disad-vantaged girls would be accepted. The surroundings she created for her students were lavish, even by western standards, which drew controversy from multi-ple quarters, but Oprah was adamant that, "If you are surrounded by beautiful things and wonderful teachers who inspire you, that beauty brings out the beauty in you."

Today the school has nearly 300 students, and is a huge success. In a country where only 14% of black girls graduate from high school, these girls buck the trend: every one of the 72 students in the first graduating class won a place at university. Graduates frequently go onto study for degrees in the US, and Oprah not only pays their tuition fees but also for their living costs, equipping them with everything they need. They call her "Mom-Oprah", and she feels very strongly that these girls are her heirs. What they achieve in life will be her proudest legacy.

When I look into the future, it's so bright it burns my eyes.

Oprah Winfrey

Lesson 37: Support initiatives you feel passionately about. Not only will they be more likely to succeed, but you will have a far greater feeling of accomplishment when they do.

Chapter 7: Leadership and Influence

In 2001, TIME magazine called Oprah "arguably the world's most powerful woman". Life listed her as the most influential black person of her generation, and called her "America's most powerful woman." *Forbes* named her as the world's most powerful celebrity in five different years (2005, 2007, 2008, 2010, and 2013), and even President Barack Obama said that she, "may be the most influential woman in the country". Whoever you speak to, at home or abroad, there is no doubt that Oprah is, and has been for three decades, one of the most influential people on the planet.

Lesson 38: People in conventional positions of power - politicians, military figures, and religious leaders - no longer exert as much influence as they did in the past. Ordinary people can spearhead significant change.

To describe Oprah's influence on middle America, *The Wall Street Journal* coined the word "Oprahfication". The term has been used in particular to refer to speaking out about personal issues, and to bringing ones private life into a public sphere. Although it was originally used to talk about public confession as a form of therapy, particularly for issues such as sexual abuse, weight problems, and a tumultuous love life, it went on to have applications in the world of politics too, encouraging politicians to speak emotionally about their problems and issues of importance to them. As *Newsweek* stated, "Every time a politician lets his lip quiver or a cable anchor 'emotes' on TV, they nod to the cult of confession that Oprah helped create."

Lesson 39: A message, delivered with conviction and emotion, will always be more effective than one based solely on rational argument.

Oprah has consistently used her position to deliberately influence public opinion, on moral and spiritual issues, as well as consumer choices. By providing a safe forum on her talk show, and encouraging guests to speak out, she was able to put previously taboo issues, such as homosexuality, on the discussion table in ordinary homes.

Although her critics have accused Oprah of blurring the lines between "normal" and "deviant" behaviour, the general view is that Oprah just made people understand that differences in sexual preference exist naturally within any given population, and talking about them is nothing to be ashamed of. As early as 1988, Oprah invited audience members to stand up and announce their sexuality on air, in observance of National

Coming Out Day. She visited a West Virginian town and publicly confronted residents paranoid about the presence of a local man with HIV, chastising them for their lack of Christian love. She also invited, and actively promoted, gay celebrities on her show, and when Ellen DeGeneres announced to the world she was a lesbian, it was to Oprah.

Lesson 40: Public attitudes are constantly in flux; there are very few issues about which opinions are completely black and white. Given time and the right figurehead, public opinions can be led in a particular direction.

Oprah has guided her fans spiritually too, both through her own teachings, and through the teachings of those she has given a platform to on her show. *Christianity Today* described her in an article, 'The Church of O', as, "a post-modern priestess—an icon of church-free spirituality." In the comic cartoon series *Futurama*, an episode set a thousand years from now has "Oprahism" as the mainstream religion.

It isn't until you come to a spiritual understanding of who you are - not necessarily a religious feeling, but deep down, the spirit within - that you can begin to take control.

Oprah Winfrey

Although Oprah herself is a Christian, she has actively promoted spirituality in all its forms. The American spiritual teacher Gary Zukav, who promotes the alignment of personality with soul to create "authentic power" and transform humanity, was invited to appear on *The Oprah Winfrey Show* on 35 separate occasions, and less than a month after the 9/11 terror attacks, she controversially aired a show called Islam 101, describing Islam as, "the most misunderstood of the three major religions". Rudy Giuliani, then mayor of New York, asked her to host the Prayer for America service at the Yankee Stadium in New York, which she did, and in 2002, George W. Bush asked her to join a US delegation to Afghanistan. Concerned that it would portray the War on Terror in a positive light, however, Oprah declined the invitation, and the trip was cancelled. Without its figurehead, the foremost opinion leader in the country, it was not worthwhile.

What God intended for you goes far beyond anything you can imagine.

Oprah Winfrey

Lesson 41: Contrary to what is often said, religion is not a personal business. People care deeply about what others

believe, and will frequently manipulate belief for political ends.

Oprah's backing in elections is, unsurprisingly, fiercely sought-after. Interestingly, she kept her political views (at least in a party political sense) to herself until 2008 when, for the first time, she openly came out and supported a presidential candidate: Barack Obama. Oprah held a fundraise for Obama at her Santa Barbara estate, joined him on the campaign trail in Iowa, New Hampshire, and South Carolina, and economists at the University of Maryland calculated that her endorsement was responsible for between 420,000 and 1,600,000 votes for Obama in the Democratic primary alone. Rod Blagojevich, Governor of Illinois, described Oprah as, "the most instrumental person in electing Barack Obama president."

Lesson 42: Democratic politics is, to a great extent, a popularity contest. He who receives the most publicity, and gets the most influential endorsements, is most likely to take home the prize.

"The Oprah Effect" has as great an impact on consumer purchases as it does on public opinion. When Oprah introduced Oprah's Book Club (see *Chapter 2:*

Television Career) in 1996, even previously obscure novels would rocket to the top of the best sellers list. According to *The New York Times*, a book recommendation by Oprah could easily generate 1 million additional sales.

The opposite is true also: if Oprah doesn't like something, and says so publicly, sales fall. During a 1996 programme about mad cow disease, Oprah was horrified by what she heard, and said she was, "stopped cold from eating another burger." Cattle prices tumbled, allegedly costing beef producers $11 million. Texas cattlemen attempted to sue Oprah for for "false defamation of perishable food" and "business disparagement", but after a two-month trial, Oprah was found not liable for damages. It was during this court case that Oprah first met Dr. Phil, and she subsequently invited him to appear on *The Oprah Winfrey Show*.

Lesson 43: Be aware of the potential impact of what you say on others. Use your platform for public good, and be prepared to defend your endorsements.

Chapter 8: Personal Life

Oprah has spent the entirety of her adult life as a public figure, speaking openly about her personal life: the whole concept of Oprahfication (see *Chapter 7: Leadership and Influence*) is, after all, about making your private life and emotions public as a means of therapy. Oprah practises what she preaches.

Relationships Oprah's romantic life, particularly in her early years, was chequered. A self-confessed promiscuous teen, she became pregnant at the age of 14, but her son died in infancy. After that, as she began to focus on education and pull her life together, she had a number of more meaningful relationships, including with a childhood sweetheart, Anthony Otey, who she met whilst still at school.

Lesson 44: Delinquent teenage years do not necessarily portend delinquent adulthood. If someone makes mistakes, especially whilst they are young, be prepared to give them a second chance.

In 1971, shortly after starting university, Oprah met William "Bubba" Taylor, her first great love. Oprah got Taylor his first job, and was absolutely besotted by him, begging him to stay with her, but when she moved to

Baltimore in 1976, he refused to follow her there. It is with some nostalgia, and lingering fondness, that Oprah says, "We really did care for each other [...] We shared a deep love. A love I will never forget."

In the late 1970s, Oprah had a succession of love affairs. She dated musician and radio host John Tesh, but according to her biographer, the couple split due to the pressure of having a mixed-race relationship. She also dated reporter Lloyd Kramer, and a married man who had no intention of leaving his wife. She has talked at length about that relationship and the desperation it made her feel, saying, "I'd had a relationship with a man for four years. I wasn't living with him. I'd never lived with anyone—and I thought I was worthless without him. The more he rejected me, the more I wanted him. I felt depleted, powerless. At the end I was down on the floor on my knees grovelling and pleading with him." When the relationship broke down, Oprah contemplated suicide, even going as far as to write a suicide note. Though she did not follow through with the idea, the emotional turmoil led to significant weight gain. Again, Oprah has spoken frankly about this issue:

> The reason I gained so much weight in the first place and the reason I had such a sorry history of abusive relationships with men was I just needed approval so much. I

needed everyone to like me, because I didn't like myself much. So I'd end up with these cruel self-absorbed guys who'd tell me how selfish I was, and I'd say 'Oh thank you, you're so right' and be grateful to them. Because I had no sense that I deserved anything else. Which is also why I gained so much weight later on. It was the perfect way of cushioning myself against the world's disapproval.

Lesson 45: Do not underestimate the emotional impact of a relationship breakdown. Whether it has happened to you, or to someone you work with, be sensitive, supportive, and allow time to start to heal the trauma.

In the early 1980s, Oprah dated Randolph Cook, film critic Roger Ebert (who encouraged her to syndicate her show, see *Chapter 2: Television Career*), and possibly also film-maker Reginald Chevalier. She got together with Stedman Graham in 1986, and although they were engaged to be married in 1992, Oprah and Stedman never actually tied the knot. They are still happily together, unmarried, and without children. They prefer to have a "spiritual union".

Lesson 46: It is fine to buck convention, in your private and professional lives. Find out what works for you and those around you, and make fulfilling those needs your priority.

Graham (born 1951) is a successful businessman and speaker, though his fame and wealth have come as result of his relationship with Oprah. He is the author of a dozen self-help books, and also has a column for *The Huffington Post*. Prior to meeting Oprah, he had a long-term relationship WBBM-TV anchor Robin Robinson.

Lots of people want to ride with you in the limo, but what you want is someone who will take the bus with you when the limo breaks down.

Oprah Winfrey

Lesson 47: Relationships don't have to be exciting all the time. Perhaps the most important thing is that you can depend on each other when things are tough. You can then enjoy the good times together even more.

Oprah's closest friend is the former news anchor Gayle King, who Oprah first met in her early twenties. Over the years, some people have suggested that Oprah and King's relationship was partly sexual in nature, but this is something which both women refute. Writing in the August 2006 issue of *O, the Oprah Magazine*, Oprah said "I understand why people think we're gay. There isn't a definition in our culture for this kind of bond between women. So I get why people have to label it—how can you be this close without it being sexual? [...] I've told nearly everything there is to tell. All my stuff is out there. People think I'd be so ashamed of being gay that I wouldn't admit it? Oh, please." As well has having a close friendship, Oprah and King have also work together extensively. King was a frequent guest on *The Oprah Winfrey Show*, and she is now an editor for *O, the Oprah Magazine*.

Lesson 48: Your friends have helped to make you the person you are today. Celebrate your friendship and support one another.

Oprah considers the writer Maya Angelou to be both a friend and a mentor, referring to the older woman as "mother-sister-friend." When Angelou turned 70 in 1998, Oprah arranged a week-long cruise for Angelou and 150 of her guests, and a decade later, to mark Angelou's 80th birthday, Oprah hosted a similarly lavish affair at the Mar-a-Lago Club in Palm Beach, Florida.

Homes Winfrey has invested some of her wealth in property, and she alternates between her different homes. Her main base, at least since having stopped filming *The Oprah Winfrey Show*, is The Promised Land, a 42-acre estate in California. She also owns homes in the US states of Colordao, Florida, Hawaii, Illinois, and New Jersey, and on the Caribbean island of Antigua.

I still have my feet on the ground, I just wear better shoes.

Oprah Winfrey

Lesson 49: Investing in property, especially across different regions, makes economic sense and the ability to call somewhere "home" gives you a sense of stability and reassurance.

Conclusion

I don't think of myself as a poor deprived ghetto girl who made good. I think of myself as somebody who, from an early age, knew I was responsible for myself, <u>and I had to make good.</u>

Oprah Winfrey

Regardless of how Oprah feels about herself, she is, for more than a generation of Americans - and African American women in particular - the ultimate pin-up girl, a woman who has made it in spite of seeming to have all of life's odds stacked against her. Her story is one of hope, and Oprah embodies, perhaps more than anyone else in the country, the American Dream.

What is indisputable, however, is that she has made it for herself. She didn't inherit her wealth, marry it, or receive any other notable handouts of money. She has earned every cent through legitimate business interests: there is not even a hint of scandal, or of wrongdoing in her past, and that in itself is remarkable.

Although Oprah's life is long and complex, there are some lessons which come through stronger than any others, and though the chances of any one of us following in her footsteps exactly are slight, by implementing them in our own lives, we can certainly improve our lot.

First of all, education is the single most effective way of lifting people out of poverty. If you cannot access education, you cannot hope to advance. It was learning to read which brought young Oprah to the attention of congregation members at her church; and a good high school and a college scholarship in Nashville which enabled her to turn her life around. Oprah understands, from personal experience, just what a different a good education can make to aspiration and lifetime achievement, and this is why she invests so much of her time, money and effort, in her educational initiatives.

Secondly, no one else is going to do it for you. If you are fortunate, there will be other people around you who encourage you, support you, teach you, and give you lucky breaks. But it is up to you to position yourself in such a way that you are able to take full advantage of them, to remain focused, and to work hard consistently.

Thirdly, and perhaps most importantly, as a person you must have credibility. If you are the face of your brand, your customers will no differentiate between what you do and what your company does. If you are providing advice, it must be of the highest quality, and this might require you to get input from experts. If you are creating a product, it must be something which others want to buy, and which they believe in. You cannot do one thing, and say something else. You must be open about your shortcomings, and the things which you have got wrong. Be prepared to accept criticism, and to learn from it. Show others that you are still human, and they will respect you all the more for it.

Lesson 50: You, and you alone, are the driving force behind your achievements. Whether or not you succeed depends on a variety of factors, but without determination, and taking responsibility for your decisions, you won't every get anywhere.

Thank you for purchasing my book! I know you could have picked from dozens of books about Oprah Winfrey, but you took a chance with mine and I appreciate it.

Made in the USA
San Bernardino, CA
18 April 2017